Molly my dear----------

it just started
raining
I love you
Jenny

minor matters.

Self-Portraits by Molly Landreth and Jenny Riffle

It's raining... I love you

ESSAY BY GENEVIEVE HUDSON

It was 1999, and they were two girls in Mount Vernon, and they were falling in love. Under the low-slung gray skies of the Skagit Valley, Jenny and Molly taught each other what it was like to be friends and lovers and young queer artists at a time when queer representation was hard to find. And since they could not see images of their life reflected in the world, they made images of themselves.

College sent them each to a different coast, so they transcribed their thoughts and feelings into playful, private love letters to one another to bridge the miles between them. They recorded their days. They collaged envelopes with fashion magazine cutouts and black-and-white photographs of each other. *My darling,* they wrote. *It just started raining. I love you.* With each picture taken, with each pining line put to paper, they added to an ever-expanding archive of young queer lives.

What comes next are the images and ephemera from that moment: documentation of first love, deep friendship. A road map, an exploration. A library of experience.

—**G.H.**

i miss you

 lovr oops jenny lou

March 2 1999
8:24 AM

Molly Landreth

Mz. Molly Mac
Landreth

1st Floor Flat
87 Buccleuch St.
Glasgow G3
GQT
Scotland

From Jenny Riffle
Bard College / Annandale-on-Hudson, NY / 12504 USA

I see two women in me, freakishly bound together, like circus twins. I see them tearing away from each other. I can hear the tearing, the anger and love, passion and pity... it requires only a bar of music to still the dislocation for a moment: but there comes the smile again, and I know that the two of us have leaped beyond cohesion."
—Anis nin

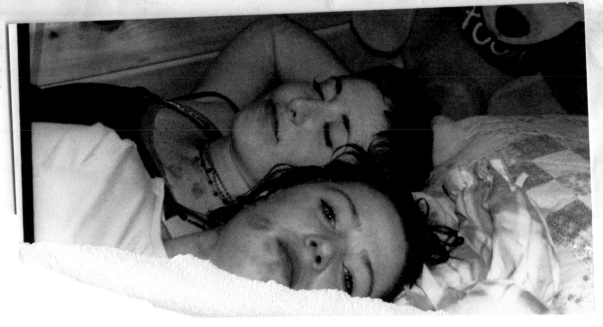

23

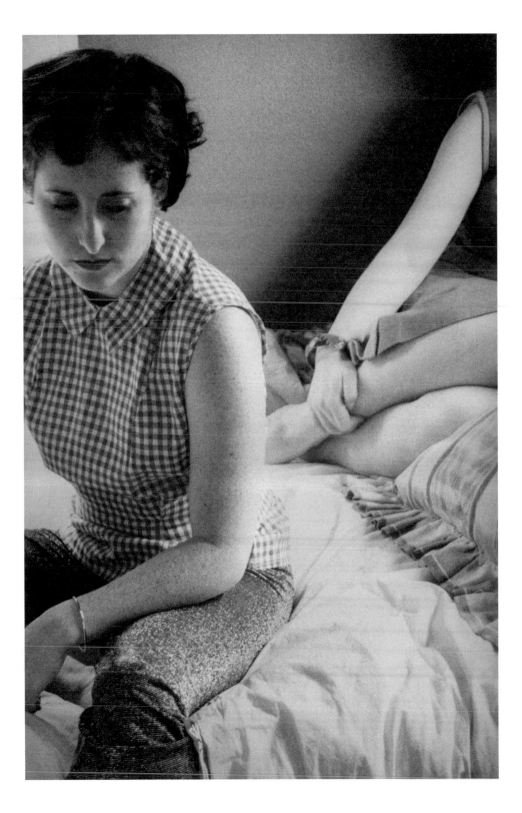

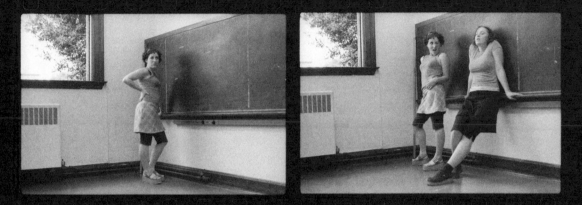

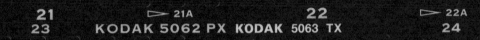

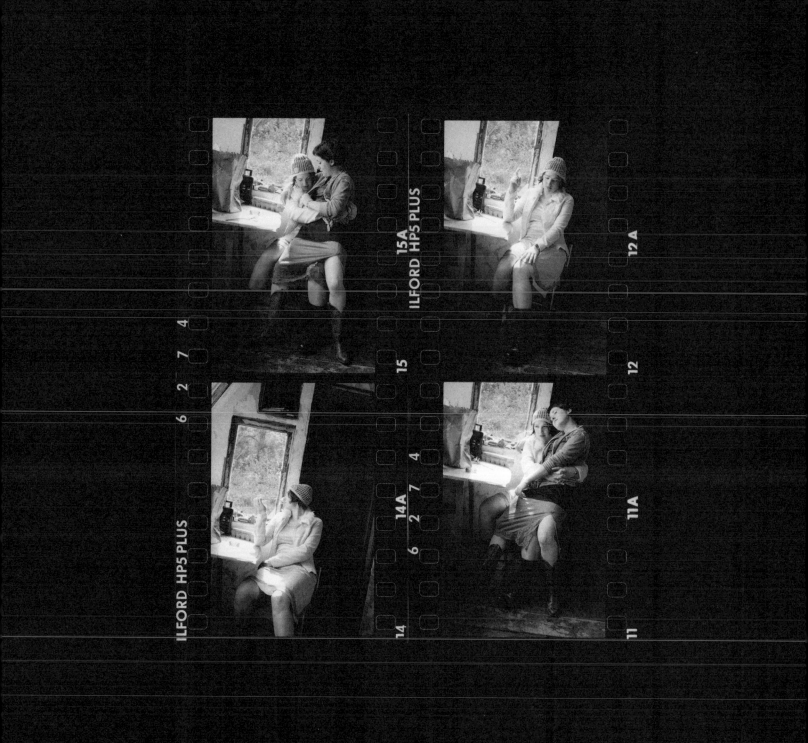

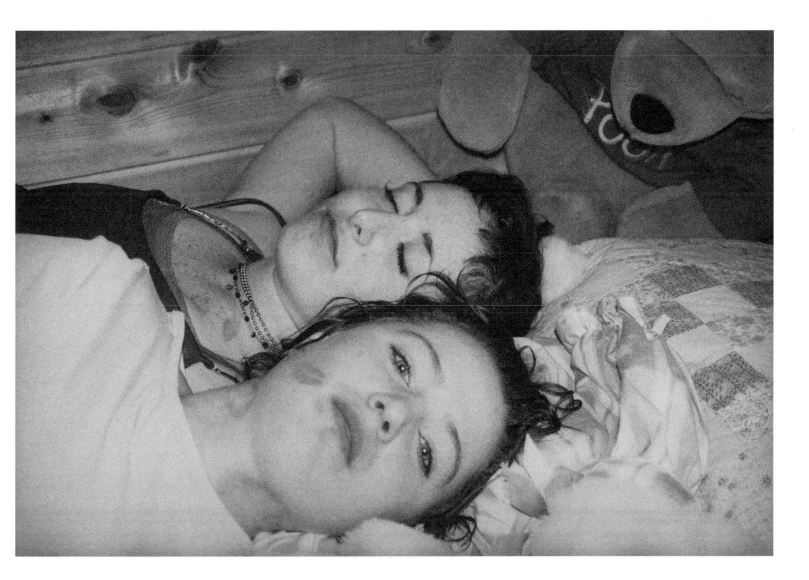

Molly my dear———————

well I found some of my photos today
under piles of blankets and such.
Today is one of those days where
it is just too hot to think. I've
been sweating all day and I just
feel like lying in a pool of water.
I keep stairing at the neighbors
pool and imagining what they
would do if they found me in it.
I'm all alone sitting in my living room
which is nice because I don't think
I've had more than an hour alone since
I got here.

It just started raining

I love you
Jenny

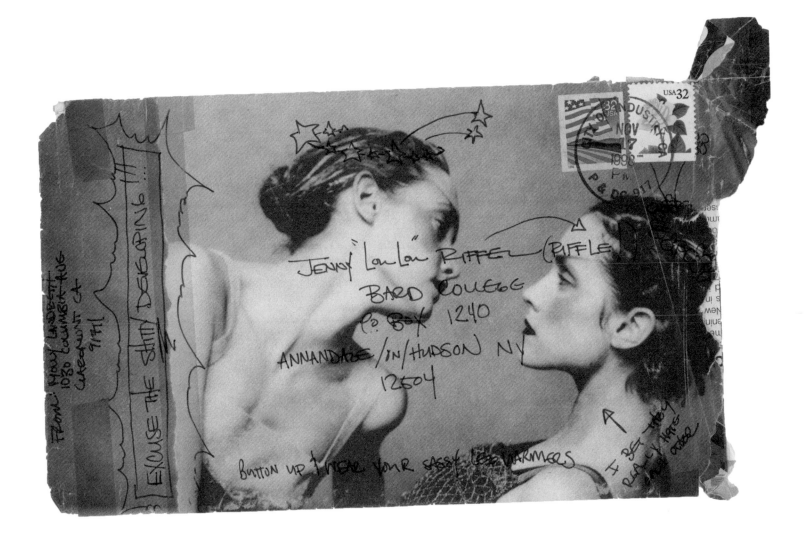

HELLO MISS Jenny - Lou. ▓▓▓▓

So HERE I AM ▓▓▓▓ IN DIGITAL "PHOTOGRAPHY" class. YEAH you REMEMBER this one well. ACTUALLY TODAY EVERYONE will BE CRITIQUING THE PORTRAITS I MADE. I ACTUALLY used THAT ONE I MADE of you / WITH YOU AND I think he liked it ... he just said ... "Hey Molly, I like those IMAGES you TURNED IN LAST WEEK". I think that MIGHT be A sign. — — MAYBE HE NEEDS GLASSES. But do you KNOW WHAT HE ALSO said ? "LOOKS like you've been getting some sleep." (BLANK STARE FROM ME - I've BEEN CRAZY) then he goes
on to explain "Yeh YA KNOW
sometimes you come IN here
you look Pretty RAGGEDY."
Ummmm heh heh heh. Yeah. How
Do you RESPOND TO THAT ?! So my
extended snoozy SPRING BREAK is officially
OVER & I'M BACK ON THE BALL, beginning
To feel the insanity of finals setting in.
So we have exactly A MONTH left of School. Fuck.
WHAT AM I GOING TO DO? RIGHT NOW WERE
LOOKING AT IMAGES OF BRIGHT COLORED
WALLS AND IT REMINDS me OF the
PICTURES you TOOK ON VERMONT. HOW
DID THOSE TURN OUT.? I CAN'T BELIEVE
THAT REALLY HAPPENED. I THINK
WANT TO DO BACK ON
DARIO'S PORAT WITH you RIGHT
NOW. The boy ACROSS FROM
ME is chewing on his
Pen so FEROCIOUSLY THAT I
think ▓▓▓ just MIGHT

"WITH THE Exception of A FEW PHOTOGRAPHERS. I DON'T LIKE OR UNDERSTAND CONTEMPORARY ART of DESIGN. BUT I REGULARLY ATTEND OPENINGS FOR THE FREE BOOZE."

Aug. 25 oregon
Salem?

Aug. 26 11:36

Jenny Riffle
Bard College Box #810
Annandale-on-Hudson
       NY 12504-5000

Molly Landreth
Dorsey Hall
Scripps College
1030 columbia Ave
Claremont CA 91711-3948

STAR ★ MOTEL

Molly Molly Molly Molly Molly Molly
Well hi, I hope everything has been
going smoothly down there in california.
It's only saturday but I found
your film in my purse and
figured I better send it to you
because if I developed it I would
eddit all the bad ones out. So this
is an excuse to write when we've
only been away from eachother for
less than 24 hours.

kiss kiss

Jenny

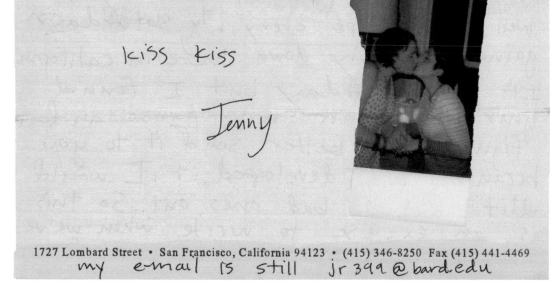

my e-mail is still jr399@bard.edu

Molita my darling,
Hello, I am (sitting) in my room mourning, I just got
back from my dad's house in Seattle and in Seattle

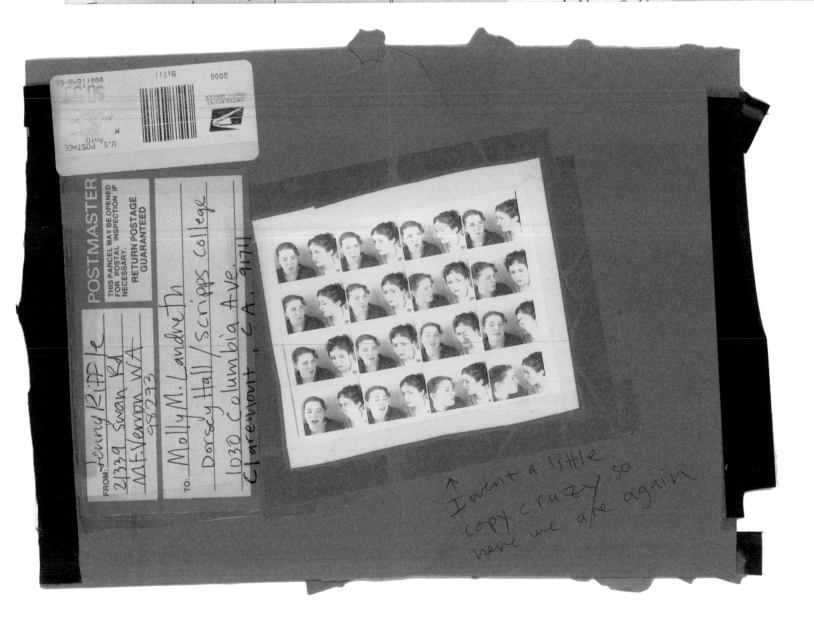

FROM: Jenny Riffle
2/329 Swan Rd
Mt. Vernon WA
98273

TO: Molly M. Landreth
Dorsey Hall / Scripps college
1030 Columbia Ave.
Claremont, CA., 91711

↑ I went a little
copy crazy so
here we are again

JENNY Lou

UMMM, I TOOK THE
E-MAIL AS AN INVITATION TO
COME OVER. I HOPE THATS
OKAY. SO I'M AT THE BAUHAUS
WAITING FOR YOU.
PLEASE JOIN ME.
MO

POSTMASTER

THIS PARCEL MAY BE OPENED FOR POSTAL INSPECTION IF NECESSARY.

RETURN POSTAGE GUARANTEED

FROM: Jenny Ripple
2/329 Swan Rd
Mt.Vernon WA
98273

TO: Molly M. Landreth
Dorsey Hall / Scripps College
1030 Columbia Ave.
Claremont, CA. 91711

↑ I went a little
copy crazy so
here we are again

Molita my darling,
Hello, I am (sitting) in my room mourning, I just got
back from my dad's house in Seattle and in Seattle
I was turning around saying "Molly?" on every
street corner. I just couldn't figure it out. Who
were you? Then I remembered that you are in
sunny California and have probably forgotten all
about little ole Jenny Lou still stuck in MV.
So I went and copied our pictures and I
pretended that your picture was you and I
just talked to you but you were not very
talkitive you just sort of staired? stared
at me with that beautiful face of yours. I
haven't seen Ross since you left. I don't know
what happened, we keep missing eachother.
Speaking of missing, I miss you ♥

love Jenny Lou
(aka Truck)

JENNY Lou
UMMM, I TOOK THE
E·MAIL AS AN INVITATION TO
COME OVER. I HOPE THATS
OKAY. SO I'M AT THE BAUHAUS
WAITING FOR YOU.
PLEASE JOIN ME.
MO

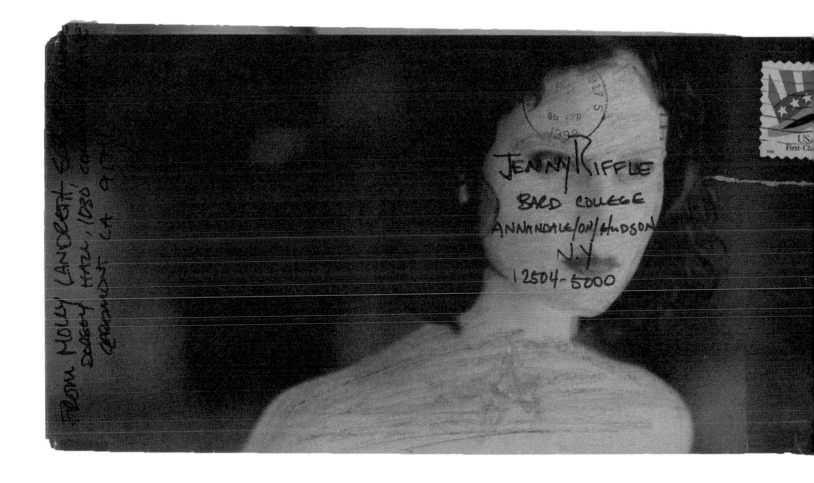

WHO WISHES TO KNOW WHAT IS TO BE ADJUDGED BEAUTIFUL AND WHO CAN TEACH IT? AND WHO CAN SET LIMITS & IMPOSE RULES ON WHAT IS SPIRITUAL? YOU MUNDANE, DRY, AND LEATHERY MEN ARE ALWAYS DEVISING RULES. THE MAJORITY WILL PRAISE YOU FOR THE CRUTCHES YOU OFFER THEM, BUT WHOEVER IS CONSCIOUS OF THEIR OWN POWER WILL RIDICULE YOU.

—CASPER DAVID FRIEDRICH (1774—1840)

93

molly,

well it's back to the type writter and back to thinking. i'm listening
to everything but the girl on my head phones because i don't have a stereo
so i feel some how separated from the world and nervous that someone is
knocking at my door but i can't hear them. all of the sudden it's fall
in new york and it's freezing. i'm still trying to figure out how i fit in
this year at bard, who am i supposed to hang out with. i feel like every
where i go i end up ignoring a part of myself, i'm a different person around
every different friend i have. eventually who ever i see the most wins an
i play their part. but i'm getting better at saying things when i should
but i still like to avoid important things, like talking to teachers and
facing up to my senior project.

my windows are stuck open and the ivy is crawling in and the machiene is
roaring outside.

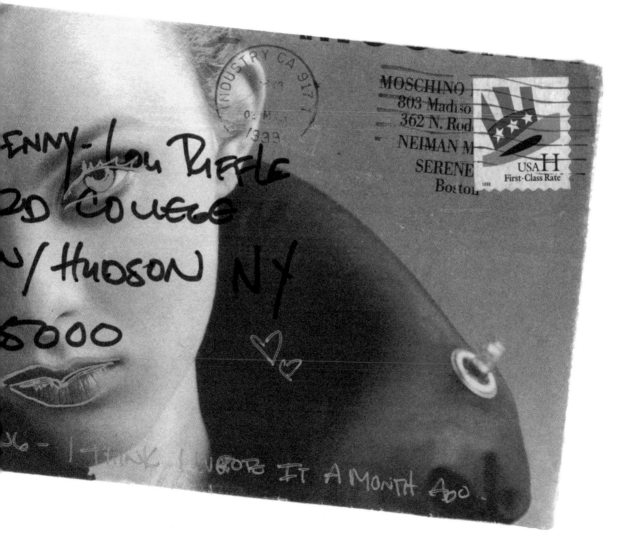

97

98

DRUNK LEZBOS

                         my darling
kudos to you for being fucking amazing, i just got your letter and i could just
  say ditto but then we've all seen GHOST and know that that just doesn'tx cut it.
       i love us molly and i love you and i know that i have a fear of lables °ops
  labels too, but it does really suck when everyone talkss about us more than we
  do. so, i don't know exactly when or how it happened but i do consider us together,
  but you, of course are free to do what x ever the hell you want, we are far far
  away from each other a big part of the year and that is some what complicating.
       together to me means that i want to be with you whenever i can.
     and i want to be with you right now but wex are able to go to school and
  keep whatever it is that we have ahd i think we kick ass, so i dont know if
  i'm making any sense but i don't know if we fit any lables , and thats good.
            so here is something i wrote sb over break

                    mine only for today
                    and tomorrow we go away
                    maybe i want you more than you know
                    and she sings along to those songs
                    and i smile and tuck that away
                    just for my memories
                    those memories i want more than anything
                    i'm sorry that i doubted my own frivolity
                    mine only for today and and
                    and tomorrow we go astray

      well i'm no poet but hey i try

                    i drive the car
                    you play the music
                    and i cried
                    i cried again because i lost
                    i lost you
                    i left you back there
                    with wax in your pretty hair
                    and the cars gone
                    and the music is lost in this new image

    so anjway kissing girls is not gross and i never liked jodie foster more than
    any great celeb,
              and it won't stop raining and i have to go to my class on the great
              depression.
       and i'm hungry, oh i had a dream the other night that i was pregnent
    should i say nightmare? anyway i was really up set and didn'treally know haw it
    happened but i was worried that you wouldn't see me anymore.

              now i really have to go to class
                 love and kisses
                      jenny
       i just re read this and thought it sounded a bit scattered, to put it plainly
    i think what we have is great and i want to keep on having it. so lets be open
    and talk if we needx to and don't worry about your sister, whatever, i miss you.
              good bye again

            JENNY
                  +
                  MOLLY

100

From
Jenny Riffle
Bard College
Annandale-on-Hudson
NY 12504-5000

Molly & JENNY
Aug. 2 1999 2:45 pm

hello my darling girl

Well it is 9:56pm on July 9 and I am trying desperately to archive my life. I purchased 2 amazing photo albums at TARGET today and have already filled them up. My parents are up stairs watching some special about the mariners. I've been thinking about you so much since you left and especially now that I'm digging back & re-organizing stuff. I feel like I've been talking to you for the past 3 hours but its really only a 2-D reflection of you & the words are all typed and not spoken. I can feel myself getting sappy ... and I want to hold back but I can't. I just really want to tell you how very much I love you. You have had such an impact on every aspect of my life and there is not a thing I do that doesn't reflect some part of you. I know that over the last few years we've had some not so happy moments ... and sometimes you confuse me so completely I feel as if I'm going insane. But what I'm really sure

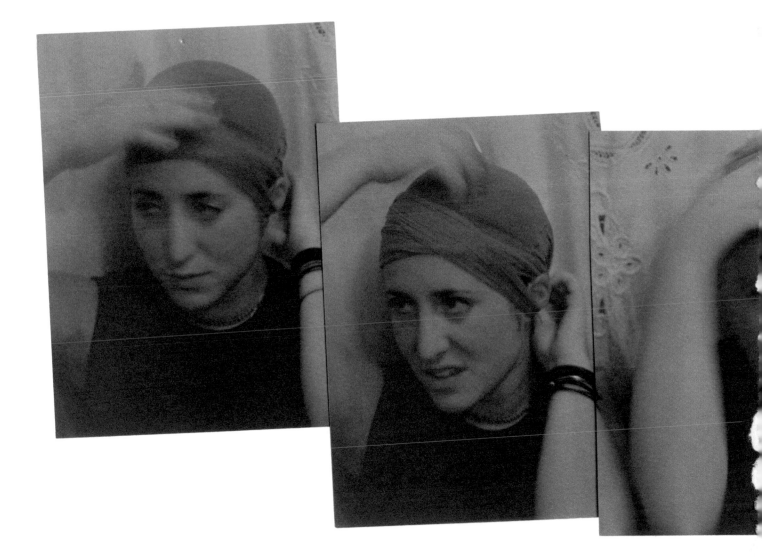

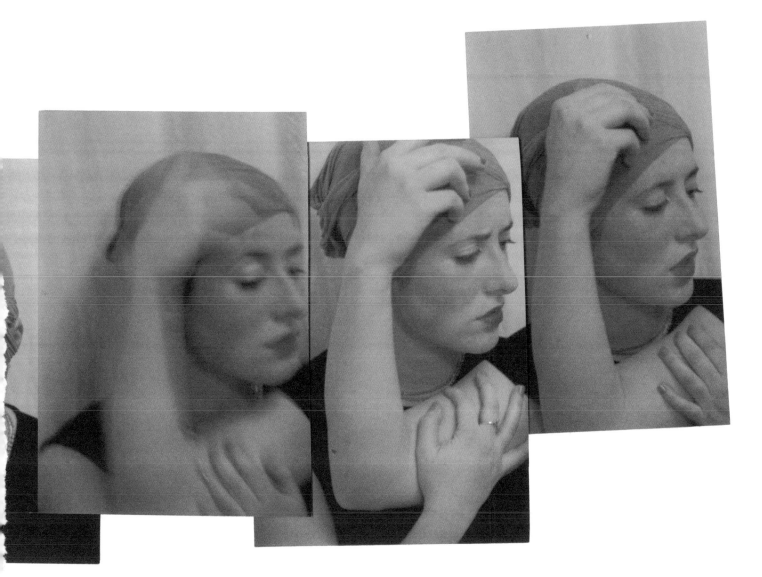

BENEATH THIS MASK, ANOTHER MASK, I WILL NOT STOP PEELING OFF ALL THESE FACES.

— CLAUDE CAHUN

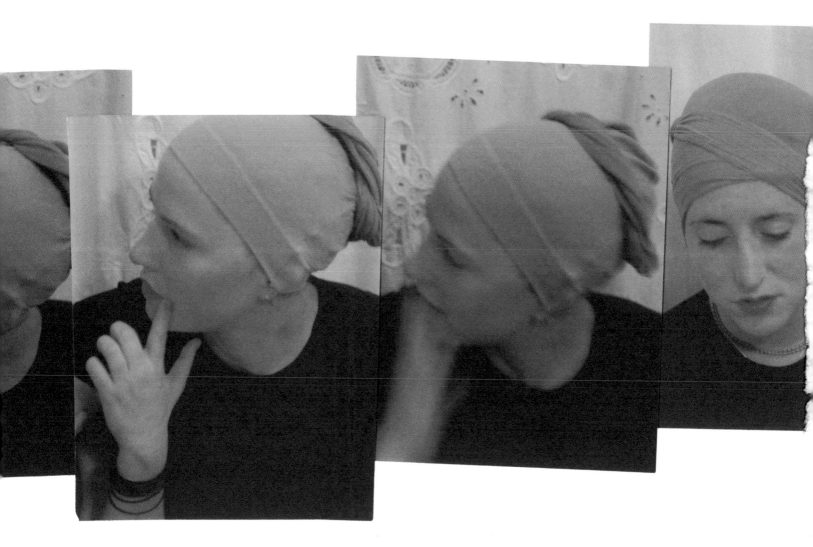

...what i'm really sure of & what i really want you to understand as well
is that loving you is the strongest emotion my body & mind has ever
experienced... and it has only grown in time. It wells up in my chest
& right before i think i can't hold anymore, that i'll explode, it
moves down to my fingertips & my eyes & my stomach, making me
feel as if i've drunk some very strong wine or (perhaps eaten
some very bad tofu :). It's the feeling that has me constantly
begging for composure.

I don't really know where i'm going with this anymore
... but i guess i just think that
everything, good & bad, that has happened between us has made
us & bit stronger, i hope. i feel as if this is turning into
an appology for heinerous unchangeable things... but that's
not what i'm sorry about. i'm just trying to relate to
you what's on my chest right now because i feel like
sometimes i don't do everything i could when we're together.
i want to wish you luck & love & everything you could think
of to wish for. i miss you & i love you & i admire you
more than i think you'll ever know.

Last semester i really didn't know how to deal with your
absence after xmas break. i tried desperately to erase you
from my mind... sort of trying to cut you cold turkey
not at all as a punishment for you, 'cause that's not it
at all. i just really needed to see my life completely without you
if i couldn't be with you. i took 6 pictures of you off of my
wall and hid them in a drawer because i was so frusterated
with you being all around me & completely untouchable. i even
started seeing Utah for a very brief while which was more of
an artistic endevor than a persuite of love (but that's a
different & brief story). i kind of went manic & had to ...

WOMEN OF THE WEST
Mary A. McCloskey, c. 1855

I had to obsessively stop obsessing about you. The thought of seeing you this last break really scared the shit out of me & although thats all I wanted to do, I felt like hiding. But of course everything was fine as it always is & you entered my life & quickly left again like a storm. But I can still feel the rumble of you inside of me. I'm really not trying to change how things are between us. That may seem hard to believe on account that I'm gushing... but really I understand that you have a life in New York & with Max & whatnot. And I'm preparing to discover excitement in L.A. I'm just saying this to get it out. I know that I need to handle things differently now. I never want to try to imagine my life without you (I never really did) even though you may be out of my eyesight.

4. THE END.
WOMEN OF THE WEST
"Mama Pushing Car at Bachelor Mine," Ouray, Colorado, May 1899
John Marshall Collection

Sometimes we don't say everything we should, sometimes we don't need to. But I felt that this needed to be said. But whatever... I love "us" in every various way shape & form. Friends, wives, lovers ... I only hope that we can continue. As cheezy as it sounds, whatever you do my heart is with you. you've captured it.

I love you so much & I hope you keep me informed on all your daily happenings... & I'll do the same. here's to 1/4 life crisis!! Remember your sunscreen, and don't smoke too much. (heh heh)

Whisper a hello to the streets of N.Y. for me.

Love...
Mo.

I'm starting again... of course there
isn't really a starting point, it is more
like the continuation of a long
conversation. Once I thought it was
starting then all of the sudden it was
ending and then it was starting again
and ending again and now I see that
its never starting or ending, it is just
always there...

Mount Vernon, Washington, 2001   107

The Urgency of the Archive

GENEVIEVE HUDSON

It was the summer of 2009 in Charleston, and I lived in an old storefront on the corner of Bogard and Rose Lane with my first-ever girlfriend. I was young and newly gay, and each day of summer seemed like the start of a story we were writing together.

The windows of our apartment were tall enough to touch the ceiling, and we had the floor-length curtains pulled shut most days to keep the heat out. The tile was a checkered black and white, and the living room, with the way the light filtered through the sheer linen, felt like a café. We drank espresso in the morning, not because it tasted good to us, but because we thought that was what French existentialists did and we wanted to channel their sophistication. We had a small orange dog who slept in our bed with us and who we took on long walks to Marion Square and up and down the uneven alleys with electric green leaves crawling up their stone sides. The sun followed us. Hard on the face and sticky, humid against our chests and arms. But the ocean was close and so cool on our skin when we needed it.

My first girlfriend and I wrote letters to each other and our friends in the spirit of Sartre and Beauvoir, hoping that one day they would be found, documenting our love and our life and our small moments, which we wanted so badly to add up to something. We read Anaïs Nin and

Frank O'Hara aloud. We watched videos of O'Hara reciting "Having a Coke with You" and felt inspired for days. I tried to draft her a poem just like his and failed. But I kept trying. I read Rilke's *Letters to a Young Poet* and she gave me a green stone that shared her name to carry in my pocket.

My first girlfriend filmed everything that summer. She took her Super-8 camera with her each time we left the house, and when I close my eyes I can still hear its whir as she put it to her eye and caught us—me and our group of friends—laughing in the big open space of a Charleston side porch. She filmed us getting tattoos and set the film to a Grizzly Bear song. She filmed us eating enchiladas. She filmed us laughing under an angel oak tree with its impressive towering limbs. She filmed friends painting the words "This Should Always Be Young" onto the side of someone's garage. Our friends took the paint across their own bodies, too. In the footage from that night, everyone is neon-colored, alive in the early morning, sipping whiskey from the bottle. A group of young gay kids whose stories my girlfriend wanted to tell.

It was a summer of firsts. It was the first time I fell in love with a woman. The first time I was part of a community of queer people who walked through the South proudly inhabiting their identities, their bodies. The first time a car full of men stopped to yell "lesbian" at me as I kissed my girlfriend goodbye on the corner of King and Vanderhorst under a palmetto tree. Their words rang in my ears all afternoon. The first time someone asked me to put a cigarette out on their arm and called it Scar Art. The first time I stayed up drinking coffee at a typewriter in a printmaking studio as my new best friend made a woodblock etching of our other friend's face. The first time someone wanted to photograph me naked.

My girlfriend was invested in the project of documentation. Everything seemed worthy of being archived, as if our everyday moments mattered not in spite of their ordinariness, but because of it. Daily tasks like eating watermelon and standing in the street shirtless in the morning heat and changing film and playing banjo were met with seriousness and cut into film and captured in Polaroids that she taped to our walls. That summer is more documented than any other time in my life. Maybe that is why the time stands out as italicized against the many memories of my life. It feels bigger, somehow.

Our youth gave us energy and mission. We needed to mark ourselves in history. We were queer and here and if we weren't represented in the world around us, we would create the representation we wanted. We wanted a canon. We wanted a museum. We started by telling the story of our lives. Our days felt precious. My girlfriend, she must have sensed how fleeting it all was, why else did she take each moment and treat it with such care? But maybe that's what you do when you are part of a marginalized group—you don't wait for others to give you the stories about your lives. You start making the stories yourself. Your life becomes the story.

It all made its way into our archive: every bad poem, every late night, every painting, every sermon on a turned-over crate. Every kiss between two boys. She staged a fight between ex-lovers. One girl walked down steep stairs of an old Victorian house and punched another girl in the face. My girlfriend filmed it all. The black eye. The bruise. Queer jealousy. We'd never seen it until then.

It all seems like one long afternoon now. Our iced coffee on the porch of Hope + Union was like a balm to the hangovers that we woke up to. I versed poems for her and recited them into the microphone, and we would edit the lines on top of our life. *It's summer in Charleston*, started one. And in that archive, it is still summer in Charleston and we are still *cold in our bones and falling in love with everyone and all these moments.*

In that archive, we are still on our way to Folly Beach to surf. I had just cut my hair, a rite of lesbian passage, and my sunglasses are still on, and our friend's shirt is still off, and he is still talking with his hands. The giant lotus flower tattoo on his ribs. The surfboard juts out between us. Our mouths are caught mid-silence-sentence. What were we singing? I don't know, but I know we were happy. In all the seriousness and the artifice and pretense, at the center of it all was our happiness. We drove up to Myrtle Beach and made a silent black-and-white of our friend walking across a mini-golf course, under giant statues of dinosaurs and across bridges where the water ran an unreal blue. We visited a video-game fortune teller. She pulled us a card. It appeared in her crystal ball.

Somewhere in my first girlfriend's hours of footage, in her boxes of developed film, in her forgotten Polaroids, there we are still. Alive in the summer of our youth. Still living. Still imbued with our firsts. Our archive has become her ephemera now; her ephemera tells our story.

Today we can look to the media and see queer life and queer stories all around us. And I wonder, if that had been the case when we were young, would my girlfriend have felt so moved to document everything? Would each moment have felt so monumental? If a canon had been readily available to us, if our experiences could be seen and heard and felt, would she have wanted so badly to archive our lives? There might have been less urgency in us all. But I'm glad the urgency was there. I'm glad that summer stands out, italicized, in all its energy and wistfulness and bliss. I'm glad I can turn to that summer and see it, the frozen scenes of us still becoming, still figuring out who we were and who we loved and who the world would let us be.

116　　Seattle, 2018

MOLLY LANDRETH (b. 1978, Walnut Creek, California; lives in Seattle) uses film cameras to create images that weave the personal with the political, while exploring concepts of community, identity, and sexuality. She received a BA in studio art from Scripps College, and an MFA in photography from the School of Visual Arts.

Landreth has focused on portraits of queer lives through personal projects and editorial work. For her series "Embodiment: A Portrait of Queer Life in America," she received the Robert Giard Fellowship from City University of New York and was named one of Humble Arts Foundation's Top 31 Emerging Art Photographers. Her work has been exhibited in galleries and festivals including the Brighton Photo Biennial, Seattle Art Museum Gallery, Jen Bekman Gallery, Leslie-Lohman Gallery, Kathleen Cullen Fine Arts, and the Camera Club of New York.

Landreth has been featured in and has photographed for the *New York Times*, *Le Monde*, the *Guardian*, *Time* magazine, *Newsweek*, the *Advocate*, *Marie Claire,* and the *New Yorker*. She is a part-time faculty member at Photographic Center Northwest in Seattle. ***www.mollylandreth.com***

JENNY RIFFLE (b. 1979, Mount Vernon, Washington; lives in Seattle) works with narrative portraiture and landscapes that explore the psychological essence of a person or place. She graduated from Bard College in 2001 with a BA in photography, and received her MFA from the School of Visual Arts in 2011. Riffle's work has appeared on NPR.org, and has been featured in numerous publications worldwide, including the *Independent*, the *Guardian*, the *New York Times*, *Telegraph*, *M: Le magazine du Monde*, *Glamour*, and *Vice*. Her first monograph, *Scavenger: Adventures in Treasure Hunting* (Zatara Press, 2015), received national attention.

Riffle's photographs have been exhibited locally, most recently at Seattle's Gallery 4Culture, and internationally, and are in several private collections, including the UBS Art Collection. Her awards include the Artist Trust GAP grant, FotoFilmic's Buschlen Mowatt Nichol Foundation Award, the Pilkington Prize, *Photo District News*'s PDN 30, and the Aaron Siskind Foundation grant. In addition to her art practice and editorial work, she teaches at Seattle's Photographic Center Northwest. ***www.jennyriffle.com***

•

Genevieve Hudson (b. 1986, Tuscaloosa, Alabama; lives in Portland, Oregon) is the author of the novel *Boys of Alabama* (Liveright, 2020). Their other books include the critical memoir *A Little in Love with Everyone* (Fiction Advocate, 2017), and *Pretend We Live Here: Stories* (Future Tense, 2018), which was a Lambda Literary Award finalist. They hold an MFA in fiction from Portland State University, and their work has appeared in *Elle*, *Oprah Magazine*, *McSweeney's*, *Catapult*, *Bookforum*, *Bitch*, Tin House online, and other publications. They have received fellowships from the Fulbright Program, MacDowell, Caldera Arts, and Vermont Studio Center. They are currently a Visiting Faculty member at Antioch University–Los Angeles's MFA Program, a freelance writer, and also work in advertising.

Minor Matters Legacy Publishers

CARYL BARON

KEN BARON

CYNTHEA BOGEL AND
JOHN STEVENSON (1944–2020)

WENDY BYRNE

JEFF DUNAS AND
LAURA MORTON DUNAS

MARINA FONT AND TOMAS NORES

LEE GRAMBUSH

DAVID HILLIARD

JOHN JENKINS III

CHRISTOPHER AND ALIDA LATHAM

LUCIA | MARQUAND

DINA MITRANI

NEW YORK PUBLIC LIBRARY, MIRIAM
AND IRA D. WALLACH DIVISION OF ART,
PRINTS AND PHOTOGRAPHS

THE SEATTLE PUBLIC LIBRARY

RICK SMITH AND GAYLE GREEN SMITH

PAT SODEN

DABI STATHAKOPOULOS

ROBERT TOMMERVIK

ANASTASIA VAN DYKE

FREDDIE YUDIN

Emily Martha Shapiro
and Sarah Coolidge

Kathy and
Howard Shapiro

Petite Galerie:
Constance Brinkley
and Kristan Parks

Tim Pfeiffer
and Housewright

Lisa Ahlberg and
Geoff Mirelowitz

Brian Allen

Kristin Allen-Zito

Tristan Anslyn

John Armstrong

Jennifer Badot

Polly Baranco and
Gemma-Rose Turnbull

Julie Bayer

Endia Beal

Kim Beil

Zack Bent

Molly Berg and
Megan Sinclair

Erica Billard

Kristen Binder

Nancy Blakey

David Boudinot

Corey Brewer

Delwyn Brooks

Anne Browning

Nicole Browning

Akvile Bukauskaite

Sera Cahoone

Bridey Caramagno

Christina Castillo

Evan Center

Katherine Cesario

Sandy Cioffi

Annabel Clark

Michelle Cleveland

Laura Close

Kelli Connell

Collen Cooke

Averi Crockett

Amy Culp

Carol Cummins

Meg Cummins

Nora Curran

Hannah Currie

Katie Dahl

Julie Dain

Dario Dalla Lasta

Natalie Dalrymple

Nat Damm

Mira Dancy

Jenny Hansen Das

Jayna Dash

Jill Dawson

John deBoer

Rachel Demy

Charlie Dibe

Joan Dinkelspiel

Julianne Duncan

Laura Enderle

Lilly Everett

Taya Faber

Michel Feaster

Andrew Fedynak

Jeff Few

Robert Foxworthy

Joe Freeman

Jeremy Funston

Stephanie Gallardo

Catherine Gaspar

Genevieve Gaudreau

Gail Gibson
and Claudia Vernia

Diane Ginthner

Steve Goldenberg

Sarah and Kim Goulter-Dunn

Kip Grant

Nessa Grasing

Wynne Greenwood

Daniel J. Gregory

Andrej Gregov

Morgan Grenier

Jay Guerrero

Eleanor Hamilton

Janet Hamilton

Lisa Hamilton

Cheryl Hanna-Truscott

Emma Hannon

Sallie Harrison

Bree Hartt

Cian Hayes

Elizabeth Hebert

Elisabeth Hein

Chris Henry

Christee Henry

Jed Holmes

Andy Holton

Thomas Holton

Kirk Hostetter

Merrilee Howard

Jordan Howland

Elisa Huerta-Enochian

Kelley Huffines

Melinda Hurst Frye and
Bronwen Houck

Scott Iffen

Ish Ishmael

Jan and Norm Jacobs

Ruth Jacobs

Stephan Jahanshahi

Lauren Jaye

Eirik Johnson

Zachary Johnson-Guthrie

Julie Johnston-Monda

Karen Jones

Chalen Kelly

Lisa Kelly

Kristi Kemp

Linda Kennedy

Matt Kennedy

Megan Kennedy

Martha Kerr

Doug Keyes

Carrie Kikuchi

Hanna King

Jessica Kinnaman

Kerri Klein

Candace Krick

Natalie Krick

Scott Kuehner

Julia Kuskin

Richard Lamanna

Natalie Lamberjack

Renee Lamberjack

Bridget Landreth

Brydie Landreth

Douglas and
Margie Landreth

Duncan Landreth

Keavy Landreth

Gus Lanza

Stephanie Lara

Adrien Leavitt

Jin Hee Lee

Jocelyn Lee

Michaela Leslie-Rule

Miriam Leuchter

Mark Levine

Gretchen Lindsay

Ilon Logan

Mugs Loudon

Sara Macel

Nancy Macko

Susan and Jon MacLaren

Kit MacPherson

Mary Grace Markham

Gregory Martin

Janice Martin

Ross Mathews

Lyn McCracken

Brie McFarland

Molly McGurn

Mud McHugh

Molly McNulty

Kim Miller

Karen Mishelof

Jeffry Mitchell

Melissa Montalto

Victoria Munro

Annie Marie Musselman

Arianna Myhre

Mary Myhre

Lance Neely

Janet Neuhauser

Lee Nichols

Deborah North

Terry Novak

Daria Okolovich

Kelly Pajek

Ann Pallesen

Margaret Pegler

Hazel Pemberton

Brad Pennella

Anthonio Pettit

Cathy and Walter Pfahl

Sally Pfeifer

Matt Phillips

Jody Poorwill

K. C. Potter de Haan

Erin Quinlevan

Stephanie Rabins

Taylor Raffa

Matt Ragen

Susan Rankaitis

Anna Ream

Kathleen Reim

John Riegler

Meghann Riepenhoff

Chris Riffle

Cliff Riffle

Conor Risch

Jessica Rose

Serrah Russell

Adair Rutledge

Jeremy Salaz

Jenny Sampson

Shannon Sandeno

Francisco Sapp

Linda Sax

Karyn Schwartz

Nick Shepard

Matthew Siltala

Katie Simmons

Mickey Simon

Mary Siple

Jane Skinner

Tara Sloan

Rafael Soldi

Sarah Solomon

The Sorelle:
Katy Jo Steward,
Mary Kongsgaard,
Martha Walton, Sue Serko,
Julie Mackoff, Ann Danieli,
Martha Kongsgaard,
Margo Keller, Patty Shelledy,
Nancy Blakey and
Eileen Butler

Bonnie Southwick

Erin Spencer

Olivia Staples

Nicole Stellner

Diana C. Stoll

Jock Sturges

Mary Virginia Swanson

Lori Talcott

Ricardo Tejeda

Kimberly Teret

Chris Terrell

Collin Terrell

Jean Terrell

Kim Terrell

Michael and Linda Terrell

Paul Terrell

Paul Terrell Jr.

Rick Terrell

Terry Terrell

Tom Terrell

Joshua Thompson

Sydney Thompson

Pam Turngren

Amy Uyeki

Eli VandenBerg

Albert Varady

Mary Vial

Patty Voros

Elisabeth Waingrow

Cass Walker

Sadie Wechsler

Winnie Westergard

Chris Williams

Sara J. Winston

Camille Wiseman

Charlotte Woolf

Loewyn Young

Paul and Connie Zickler

Ron Zuckerman

Jennifer Zwick

Reflections

One afternoon in the summer of 1999, Molly and I saw a field of daisies near her parents' house, and it reminded us of the professional family portraits hanging in the hallways of our childhood homes. So we tried to make our own family portrait **(page 1)**. I remember posing for the camera, and how ironic and funny I thought my pose would be, with my hand under my chin—poking fun at all the family portraits that had come before, with their studied poses. Looking back now, this image has lost some irony and gained some nostalgia. In that way it really has become our own family portrait. I realize now that we were trying to see what two women together would look like in such a traditional portrait pose, because we had never seen a portrait like that hanging in a family home. What those poses represented was something very real and meaningful: a family, a couple, a home. And we wanted to see ourselves in those roles.

The narratives in our images were never discussed beforehand. We always set up the tripod and the camera with one of us in the scene and one of us behind the camera (we traded off who played which part), and once we hit the timer on the shutter, the one behind the camera would run into the scene and do something—whatever came to mind in that instant. What one did activated the other to react and the photograph was captured. The photograph on **page 21** in this book has always been one of my favorites because of the dramatic narrative created. I love the way Molly is holding me and how we are both looking off-camera to some unknown scene. It is like the cover of a romance novel—overly dramatic, but romantic nonetheless.

Most of the images in this book were printed back in 1999, sometimes on the day when we made the photographs. We had access to a darkroom in Seattle in Molly's uncle's studio, where we would go at night when everyone else had gone home. We would excitedly develop the negatives, pick our favorites, and make prints of them. Looking back at those negatives today, I see how overprocessed they are, but we loved the high contrast and rough edges— they called to mind fashion and punk zines of the '90s. It has been amazing to discover photographs we never printed until going back through our

contact sheets for this book. One of my new favorites **(page 41)**, which we never printed back when it was made, feels so spontaneous and candid. It's like looking at a photograph of my grandparents, young and in love.

Occasionally Molly and I found ourselves wearing the same outfit. On one particular day, Molly showed up at my place and we decided to sneak into a big abandoned school building to take photographs **(pages 62–67)**. I don't remember thinking at the time that we looked like schoolgirls, but looking back it's as if we dressed up specifically for these scenes. It was like we got to act out all the years of school we had together, but now playing girls in love. No one was out in our high school, and this was a time before clubs like the Gay-Straight Alliance existed, so in a sense this was us re-creating our own history.

—Jenny

In the summer of 1999 I learned how to drink coffee, as Jenny and I sat at the A&W Drive-In **(pages 17–19)** in Anacortes, Washington, about fifteen minutes from where we grew up. It smelled like French fries and sounded like the endless hum of homemade milkshakes.

Arriving back home from college for summer vacation that year, our hometown felt at once comforting and cinematic in its small-town-ness. At this point in time, sipping coffee in a diner and making future plans was the closest we came to going out on a date. I remember Jenny telling me that she had started drinking coffee in New York. "The trick is to put enough cream and sugar in it so it doesn't taste like coffee." For the rest of that summer I craved the taste of watered-down diner coffee because it tasted just as sweet and rebellious as Jenny's lips.

Jenny and I have very close bonds with our siblings; we both have sisters who are younger than us by twelve years. By now the age differences have dissolved, but during the summer of 1999 the gap in age created room for unspoken narratives and tensions in various photographs, especially since we were not yet out to our families. For one series of images **(pages 22–28)**, we brought my sisters Keavy (fifteen) and Brydie (seven) along for a "photo adventure," dressed up in my clothes. At one point we found ourselves in downtown Anacortes, on a side street off of the main part of town **(page 24)**. Setting the camera up on a tripod, we didn't say much, just instructed my sisters to "look into the camera and don't smile." We didn't know what we were acting out, but I remember feeling tough and protective, like runaways, or a strange girl gang—like in *The Outsiders*. We had a secret and so much to protect. These have always been my favorite images from the whole series.

On one occasion, Jenny and I had just picked up my little sister from her Highland dance lesson, and we were taking her home **(pages 29–31)**. Our friend Ross was following behind in his car so we could all hang out that evening. Suddenly, Jenny and I saw this great expanse of trees and knew that we needed to make a photograph. We motioned to Ross to pull over. I remember him muttering, "You girls . . ." and I love that you can see his car keys peeking out of his hand. Looking back now, I see that, without really understanding it at the time, Jenny and I were slyly using men in our photographs to point to the ever-present male gaze, and a societal expectation to conform to a heteronormative life. Here we used our friend Ross (who is now, ironically, a gay celebrity) as a straight-man foil for our own queer desire.

One day a carnival popped up in the parking lot of our local mall. Poof! Overnight magic—fried food, and rusty Ferris wheels, right next door to Denny's. Immediately Jenny and I put on our best carnival outfits and went to make photographs **(pages 41–45)**. There was something deliciously secretive and exciting about our relationship that was amplified when we were in public, in non-queer spaces **(pages 42–43)**. I loved that people knew there was something going on between us, but couldn't identify what. Sisters? Twins? The mirroring that was happening between us, as we worked to find and shape our identities, was undeniable. Now I understand that this ambiguity shielded us from some of the harsher realities that can go along with coming out in a small town. That sort of "passing" privilege is something I am gaining awareness of only now, in retrospect. It is something I continue to navigate to this day.

—**Molly**

Acknowledgments

Thank you to all the people who have lent their talent, support, and guidance throughout this book-making process; Kristin Allen-Zito, Timothy Atticus, Sarah Coolidge, Michelle Dunn Marsh, Genevieve Hudson, Ish Ishmael, Natalie Krick, Ann Pallesen, Chris Riffle, Cliff Riffle, Kathy and Howard Shapiro, Emily Shapiro, and Jock Sturges.

—**J.R.**

Thank you to my parents, Bridget and Duncan; to my sisters, Keavy and Brydie; and to my ex-wife, Kennedy, for your unwavering support, love, and encouragement through the years. Doug Landreth, thank you for your mentorship and for giving me the keys to your darkroom. Michelle Dunn Marsh, and Genevieve Hudson, thank you for your collaboration and talent. I dedicate this book to Beau. May you know great love and stay true to yourself along the way.

—**M.L.**

It's Raining . . . I Love You is published by Minor Matters:
Michelle Dunn Marsh, publisher
Steve McIntyre, partner and platform chief
Diana C. Stoll, text editor
Co-Publishers listed on pages 119–23

ISBN: 978-1-7321241-8-9
Library of Congress Control Number: 2020943726

FIRST EDITION 10 9 8 7 6 5 4 3 2 1

Founded in 2013, Minor Matters is a collaborative publishing platform for contemporary art, bringing books into being with the support and action of our audience. We focus on work that articulates the surface of life, bringing insight and cadence to the worlds we occupy. **To learn more or purchase other titles please visit: www.minormattersbooks.com**

Minor Matters Books LLC, Seattle | New York
(206) 856-6595 | (212) 729-3235 |
info@minormattersbooks.com

MINOR MATTERS would like to thank all our Legacy Publishers and the Co-Publishers of *It's Raining . . . I Love You*, particularly the Foto Femmes, the community of PCNW (especially Eirik Johnson), and Emily Martha Shapiro. Thank you to Marteinn Jónasson, *F-Stop* magazine, Amanda Carter Gomes and *The Fold* magazine, alumni/ae associations at Bard College and the School of Visual Arts, Justin Tindall at It Gets Better Project, and gay-owned Seattle businesses that uplift the entire community here. Special thanks to Genevieve Hudson for an insightful essay. Minor Matters continues to create books for our present, and our future. They include: Silvia Tornga McIntyre, Christian and Madison McIntyre; Alistaire, Jackie, Xavier, and Kai Marsh; Otto Van Dyke; Kerlin and Jesse Pyun; Zara and Nina Park; Jasper and Thea Layman; and the next gen in Eire and Oz.